Other Books & CDs by Bill Ferguson

The Mastery Of Life Audio Course
8 audio CDs and a 90 page workbook

A step-by-step process for having life work

This course is about creating miracles. It,s about learning, healing, taking action and developing the skills you need to have your dreams come true.

How To Heal A Painful Relationship And If Necessary, Part As Friends
Paperback or 2 CDs

Learn how to end conflict, heal hurt, be free of resentment, and restore love in any relationship.

Heal The Hurt That Sabotages Your Life
Paperback or 2 CDs

Be free of the hidden inner issues that destroy love and create suffering.

How To Divorce As Friends And Maybe SaveYour Marriage
4 Cassettes or 2 CDs

This audio set walks you through the process of healing your relationship, one human being to another.

Miracles Are Guaranteed

A Handbook for Living

A STEP-BY-STEP GUIDE TO
RESTORING LOVE, BEING FREE, AND
CREATING A LIFE THAT WORKS

BILL FERGUSON

Return to the Heart
P.O. Box 541813
Houston, TX 77254

www.masteryoflife.com

Return to the Heart
P.O. Box 541813
Houston, Texas 77254
U.S.A.
(713) 520-5370
www.masteryoflife.com

Copyright © 2006 by Bill Ferguson

Cover design by Mark Gelotte

Library of Congress
Control Number: 2005910555

Second Edition

ISBN 1-878410-38-5

Made in the United States of America

This book is dedicated to Sue: my wife, my partner, and my best friend.

CONTENTS

CONTENTS

CHAPTER 1

CREATE THE EXPERIENCE OF LOVE

You can create a life of miracles. This may seem impossible but it's not. This is actually the natural state. You lived this way when you were a young child, but lost it in the process of growing up. Now you can get it back.

You can set yourself free inside and have your life be the exciting adventure it once was. You do this by creating something called the experience of love.

When the experience of love is present, life is a joy. You are happy and alive. You have inner freedom and peace. You feel good about yourself, your life, and everyone around you. You are confident, creative, and very effective.

You can flow with whatever happens. You see life clearly and know what needs to be done. You radiate a very positive energy, life works wonderfully, and great things happen.

This is the experience of love. This is also where miracles take place.

The presence or absence of this state may seem to be a function of what happens around you, but it's not. It's a function of how you relate to what happens. In other words, it's a function of you.

You create or destroy the experience of love by how you relate to the world around you. A good way to see this is to look at relationships.

How do you feel when someone genuinely accepts and appreciates you? Doesn't this feel great? Of course it does. You feel better about yourself and better about life. You also feel better about the person who accepts and appreciates you.

The same thing happens when you accept and appreciate someone else. That person automatically feels better about life and better about you.

By giving acceptance and appreciation, you create the experience of love.

Now look at the opposite. How do you feel

when someone is non-accepting, critical, or controlling towards you?

Instantly, the experience of love disappears. You get hurt and upset. You put up your walls of protection and automatically resist the person who treats you this way.

The same thing happens when you are non-accepting, critical or controlling toward someone else. That person gets upset, puts up his or her walls of protection, and becomes critical and resentful toward you.

Every time you interact with another person, or with life itself, you either create love or destroy love – and whatever you give comes right back.

When you give acceptance and appreciation, you create the experience of love and great things happen around you. When you give non-acceptance, you destroy love and negative things happen around you.

Literally, you determine what happens around you by how you relate to life. If you want your life to be full of miracles, put your focus on creating the experience of love. You do this by giving the gift of acceptance and appreciation.

Unfortunately, this is much easier said than done. Some people and certain areas of life are very difficult to accept.

Fortunately, non-acceptance is an illusion. Have you ever tried to change someone? Have you ever been successful? Not likely.

How many times have you tried to change someone and the person got worse? This is much more likely. Just look at how you feel when someone tries to change you. How do you feel about changing? Not very interested, are you?

Find someone in your life that you can't accept. Notice that this person has a particular view of life and a particular way of behaving. Notice that this person is exactly the way he or she is without any regard for how you feel about it.

What we fight is the truth. At any moment, the people in your life are the way they are, your circumstances are the way they are, and you are the way you are.

Everything may change tomorrow, but at this moment, your life and the people in it are exactly the way they are.

When you fight the truth of the way someone is, you destroy the experience of love. You get upset and close down. All you can do is fight, resist, hang on, and withdraw.

The other person then gets upset and becomes non-accepting and critical toward you. Then you get more upset and more critical toward the other person. Then the other person becomes more critical toward you.

Without knowing, you create a cycle of conflict: a cycle of resisting, attacking, and withdrawing from each other. This cycle goes on and on without either person ever noticing his or her role in the conflict.

This cycle of conflict is present in any relationship that isn't working. It's also present in any area of your life that isn't working. There is something that you are resisting. This area of life then resists you in return.

By resisting, you create opposition and resistance against yourself. It's like a law of physics. The very act of resisting magnifies and gives power to whatever you resist.

Imagine four yellow balloons on the ceiling above you. Now, whatever you do, don't think about them. You just thought about them. Don't do that. Stop.

Notice what happens when you resist the yellow balloons. You keep thinking about them. In fact, you can hardly think about any thing else. Resisting the thought of yellow balloons gives the thought power and keeps it alive.

The same thing happens with anything you resist. By your resisting, you create more of the very circumstances that you are attempting to avoid.

Look at the areas of your life that work effortlessly. These are areas where you can flow. There is no resistance. You see life clearly and are very effective.

Now look at the areas of life where you suffer. These are areas where you can't flow. By resisting, you keep these areas of life from working. If you could let go of the resisting, these areas would clear up.

Difficult situations need action, not resisting. When you resist, you create a state of fear, upset, and tunnel vision that destroys your ability to see what needs to be done.

So why do we resist? We resist so we don't have to feel all the suppressed hurt from the past that is being reactivated by our circumstances.

In an automatic, subconscious avoidance of this hurt, we fight, resist, hang on, and withdraw. This in turn destroys love and sabotages our lives.

Until you heal this suppressed hurt from the past, you will continue to resist. Your life will be full of struggle and the happiness that you seek will elude you forever.

Fortunately, it's possible to heal this hurt. You can have the experience of love in every relationship and in every aspect of your life. This book will show you how.

First, you will learn how to heal your hurt and flow with life. Then you will learn how to create an environment where miracles are guaranteed.

ACTION TO TAKE

- Recall a time when you had the experience of love. Notice what your life was like. Notice how free and alive you felt. Notice how you felt about yourself and the world around you.

- At any moment, your life is the way it is whether you like it or not. Notice what happens to the experience of love when you resist the way life is. Now notice what happens to the experience of love when you are at peace and appreciate life.

- Notice how you have created or destroyed the experience of love in your life.

- Ask yourself these questions: Are you willing to have the experience of love in every relationship and in every aspect of life? Are you willing to have your dreams come true?

- Make creating the experience of love the highest priority in your life. If you do this, everything else will handle itself. Use this book to learn how.

CHAPTER 2

HEAL THE HURT

The moment you get upset, the experience of love disappears. You close down inside. You get tunnel vision and lose your ability to see clearly. All you can do is fight, resist, hang on, and withdraw. This in turn makes your situation worse.

We think that upsets are caused by what happens, but they are not. Upsets are caused by fighting and resisting what happens.

Find a time in your life when you were upset. Now notice what would happen to the upset if you were totally at peace with what happened. There would be no upset.

If someone spills a glass of water on you, you are going to be wet, and how you feel about it is totally irrelevant. You are still wet.

If you are at peace with being wet, you will have peace of mind. You will see your situation clearly and can see what needs to be done. You will be very effective.

If you fight being wet, you are going to be upset, and the more you fight being wet, the more upset you are going to be. But the upset is not the result of being wet, the upset is the result of fighting and resisting being wet.

The moment you take away the fighting and resisting, the upset disappears, and your effectiveness returns.

Notice that different people get upset at different things. If upsets were truly caused by what happened, then each person would react in exactly the same way. Obviously, this doesn't happen.

In one of our workshops we do an exercise that demonstrates this. We tell everyone to close their eyes and relax. Then we have them notice whatever emotions they experience when we say certain words. We say words like "You're fired," "I love you," "You can't do anything right," and "I don't love you anymore."

Each person has a totally different reaction to whatever words we say. When we say "you're fired," one person may feel relieved while another feels devastated. When we tell them "I love you," one person may feel warm and happy while another feels sad or afraid.

Each person reacts in a different way because each person has a different set of suppressed emotions that get triggered. The more powerful these emotions, the more they run our lives.

The most destructive emotions come from our childhood. These emotions are the child-hood hurt of feeling worthless, not good enough, not worth loving, a failure or some other form of feeling not okay.

It's not the truth that we are this way. It's just a suppressed childhood hurt, but it's a hurt that totally runs our lives. As we run from this hurt, we destroy the experience of love. We sabotage our relationships, our careers, and our dreams.

To see some of the suppressed emotions in your life, notice what happens the moment you get upset. Instead of looking at your circum-stances, look at what happens inside of you. Notice the immediate and powerful surge of emotions that come forth when you get upset.

When we get upset, we think we are avoiding certain circumstances but we're not. We are avoiding the powerful emotions that these circumstances reactivate.

As we run from these feelings, we create havoc in our lives.

Any circumstance that triggers this hurt is considered a threat. In an automatic, subconscious attempt to avoid this threat, we fight, resist, hang on, and withdraw. This in turn destroys the experience of love and makes our lives more difficult.

If you could separate your circumstances from your feelings and allow yourself to feel this hurt from your past, the feelings would lose power and go away.

A good way to see this is to look at how little children handle hurt. When a young child gets hurt, the child cries. Then, when the crying is over, the hurt is all gone.

Children are masters at healing hurt because they do something we don't notice. Instead of fighting their hurt, they feel it willingly. This allows the hurt to run its course. It comes and then it goes.

This is the natural process for healing hurt. When you allow yourself to feel your hurt willingly like a child, it loses power and goes away.

Unfortunately, we have been taught to avoid our hurt. Instead of feeling it willingly, we have been taught to fight it. We are told, "Big boys and girls don't cry." "If you want something to cry about, I'll give you something to cry about."

We learn to suppress our hurt which then circumvents the natural healing process. Instead of flowing with the hurt and letting it go, we fight the hurt and keep it inside.

We try to push the hurt away, but we can't. The hurt isn't outside of us. It's inside. So, in our attempt to push the hurt away, we actually push the hurt deeper inside.

We then spend the rest of our lives running from the very hurt that we have suppressed. We run from this hurt, but we can't get away from it. As long as we have this hurt, it is going to get triggered. We are going to feel the hurt over and over.

Our only choice is how we are going to feel our hurt. When we feel the hurt willingly like a child, the hurt comes and goes. When we feel it unwillingly, the hurt turns into pain and stays.

To see this in your life, find a time when you were hurt and you allowed yourself to cry. Then, after you cried your last tear, you felt a wonderful freedom. This will be a time when you felt your hurt willingly.

Now recall a time when you were hurt, you experienced it as being painful, and the hurt seemed to stay. This is a hurt that you felt unwillingly.

When you feel your hurt because your circumstances are making you feel it, the healing process can take forever. You can cry hours a day for months with little or no relief.

If you take the same hurt and feel it because you want to, because you choose to, the healing process will be very fast.

So feel your hurt willingly like a child. Feel it because you want to, because you want to reach in, grab it, and pull it out.

Keep telling yourself, "It's okay to feel the hurt. It's okay." Let the hurt come and let it go. Cry as hard as you can. Crying is the most powerful tool for releasing hurt.

If you feel the hurt, but there aren't any tears, fake the tears. Get into the emotion and exaggerate the hurt. Experience it as deeply as you can. Faking the tears can be just as effective as the real tears.

You may notice certain thoughts as you cry: "Why did she do this?" "Why can't she love me?" Let your thoughts guide your crying. Cry each thought. Then move to the next one. Let the hurt take over. Let it come and let it go.

Do everything you can to get this suppressed hurt out of you. Then go through life looking for opportunities for more healing. Whenever you get upset, go to the hurt that fuels the upset and dive into it. Feel your hurt because you want to, because you want to set yourself free.

The more you release your suppressed hurt, the less hurt there will be to get triggered. You will be more able to flow with life and you will be more able to have your dreams come true.

In the next two chapters, you will learn how to find and heal the deeper, childhood hurt of feeling worthless, not good enough, not worth loving, failure, and more.

This deeper hurt is referred to as a "core issue."

ACTION TO TAKE

- Notice what happens when you get upset. Instead of looking at the circumstances, notice what happens inside. Notice the powerful surge of emotion that gets reactivated.

- Now notice how much you avoid feeling this emotion. Notice how you try to force life to be a particular way so you don't have to face this suppressed hurt from the past.

- Notice the damage you have caused in your life by avoiding this suppressed hurt.

- Be like a young child and feel your hurt willingly. Feel it because you want to, because you want to reach in, grab it, and pull it out. This is the key to healing your hurt.

- Go through life looking for opportunities for more healing.

CHAPTER 3

FIND YOUR CORE ISSUES

Each of us have several core issues that destroy love. These issues sabotage our relationships, our careers, and keep our dreams from coming true.

They destroy our aliveness and our peace of mind. They are the root of our hurt, our upsets, and all our self-sabotaging behavior. These issues are issues that we have with ourselves.

When we were born, we were full expressions of love. Unfortunately, we were born into a culture that destroys love. As a result, we soon experienced a very painful, shocking loss of love from both our parents and our friends.

As a young child, the only way we could

explain these painful losses of love was to blame ourselves. Clearly, something was wrong with us. Why else would people treat us the way they do?

We then decided that we were worthless, not worth loving, a failure, not good enough, or some other form of being "not okay."

This wasn't the truth, but in a moment of deep hurt, it became our truth. This was the only explanation that made any sense at the time.

The loss of this love and the notion that we were not okay was so painful that we spend the rest of our lives running from this hurt.

Anything that triggers this hurt then be comes a threat. In an automatic, subconscious attempt to avoid this threat, we fight, resist, hang on, and withdraw. This in turn sabotages our lives.

We become defensive, full of fear and upset. We get tunnel vision and we act in a way that makes our situation worse. We do tremendous damage to our lives without ever noticing our role in the problem.

The automatic, subconscious avoidance of this hurt is responsible for all the suffering in your life. It is responsible for all your upsets and all your self-sabotaging behavior patterns. Every area of your life that doesn't work can be traced directly to this hurt.

The irony is that the more you fight and resist these feelings of being not okay, the stronger they become and the more they run your life. When you run from failure, you create failure at every turn.

There is nothing you can do to get rid of worthless, failure, or whatever your core issue is. You can't get rid of it because everything you do to push it away gives it more power.

However, you can make peace with these aspects of being human and you can get to the place where they lose their relevance. You can get to the place where you can say, "Yes. I'm worthless. So What? I'm also worthy."

In the "So what?" the core issues lose power and disappear.

The first step in healing this hurt is to find as specifically as possible, what the hurt is. What are the characteristics that you avoid and resist?

Find Your Core Issue.

These core issues will always be the childhood hurt of feeling worthless or some other form of "not okay." It's not the truth that you are this way; it's just an old hurt. The truth and the hurt are totally separate.

So don't look to see if you are this way. You're not. Look to see if it would be painful if you really were this way. The more painful this would be, the closer you are to the hurt that runs your life.

Look for the words of "not okay" that are the most painful. Are you worthless, not good enough, not worth loving, inferior, or a failure?

While you are looking, notice if there are any words of "not okay" that you deny being. "I know I'm not worthless." "I'm not a failure." The more you deny being a certain way, the closer you are to your hurt.

You may find lots of painful words, but for now, look for the ones that hurt the most. The following sections will show you where to look.

Make a list of all your major upsets.

Every time you have been upset will be a

time when your hurt has been triggered. That's why you got upset.

Write down every upset you can think of. Then go to the hurt that's under each upset and find what those circumstances say about you.

For example, if someone leaves you, that may say that you are not worth loving. If you are fired from a job, that may say that you are a failure or not good enough.

Make a list of all your upsets. Then write down the hurt that's under each upset. See if you can find a theme that runs through all of them.

How is your relationship with your parents?

If you had a difficult relationship with one or both of your parents, this is probably where your hurt began.

Go back in time and put yourself in the hurt that you experienced as a child. What did your parents imply about you in their words and actions?

Did they say that you were worthless or not good enough? Find the words that most accurately describe the hurt that you experienced as a child.

Now notice how painful it would be if your parents were right about you. You really are this way. The more painful this is, the closer you are to your hurt.

What do you resist in your parents?

Any characteristic that you resist in another person is an aspect of you that you resist in yourself. Find the characteristics that you resist in your parents. Then notice how you would feel if you were this way.

What are you driven toward?

We are never driven toward something. We are driven away from something. For example, if someone is driven to succeed, that person is running from failure. If someone has to be loved, that person is probably running from the hurt of feeling not worth loving.

Find what you are driven toward and look for the opposite.

What are the areas of your life that don't work?

Any area of your life that doesn't work is

an area where you are resisting. You are resisting, because this area of life triggers your hurt.

List the primary areas of your life that don't work. Then find the hurt that you are avoiding. What do these circumstances say about you?

What are your fears?

Make a list of all your fears and for each fear, find the hurt that you are avoiding. What would it say about you if your fear came true? What would you have to feel? Find the hurt that is under each fear.

Review a list of common core issues.

Look over the following list of core issues and find which words are the most uncomfortable. For each word, notice how it would feel if you really were this way. The more painful a particular word, the more it runs your life.

unlovable
undesirable
not worth loving
not good enough
    to be loved
not worth respecting

don't have what it
    takes to be loved
worthless
have no value
have deficit value
flawed

no good
not good enough
inadequate
inferior
less than
useless
a nothing
insignificant
unimportant
don't count
don't matter
disposable
a throwaway
a nobody
a loser
a failure
underachiever
don't measure up
can't cut it
don't have what it
   takes
incompetent
screwed up
something is wrong
   with you

can't do anything
   right
stupid
unstable
defective
not acceptable
weak
a coward
irresponsible
unreliable
lazy
self-centered
inconsiderate
selfish
dishonest
bad
wrong
evil
repulsive
heartless
a horrible person
ugly
fat
a slut
just like your parents

What is your hurt?

You may find several words that are painful. For example, you may have the hurt of feeling not good enough, not worth loving, and of being a failure.

You need to heal all of these core issues, but for now, find the words that hurt the most. For most people, the bottom line hurt is the hurt of feeling worthless. What is the hurt that runs your life?

ACTION TO TAKE

- Every one of us has a suppressed hurt from the past that sabotages our lives. This hurt is childhood hurt of feeling worthless, not worth loving, not good enough, or some other form of feeling "not okay." Use this chapter to find what your hurt is.

- Remember that you are not looking for the truth. You are looking for the hurt. The truth and the hurt are never connected. Look for the hurt.

- Find the words of "not okay" that are the most painful. The more painful the words, the closer you are to your hurt.

- If you deny being a certain way, you have probably found your hurt. You wouldn't want to deny it unless you had an issue with it.

CHAPTER 4

MAKE PEACE WITH THE DRAGON

There is nothing you can do to get rid of worthless, not worth loving, failure, or whatever your issue is. In fact, everything you do to get rid of it gives it more power.

You cannot get rid of these core issues, but you can make peace with them. You can get to the place where you can say, "Yes. This is an aspect of me. So what? I'm also the opposite."

As you get to the place of "So what?" the issue loses power and disappears. But unfortunately, you can't just jump to "So what?" You must first face the dragon and realize that, like it or not, this is an aspect of you.

By facing the dragon and allowing yourself to feel the hurt of being this way, the hurt loses power. You then discover that being this way is truly, "So what?"

The moment this happens, your whole life begins to change. You see life more clearly and you become far more effective.

Finding and healing this hurt is the key to creating a life that works. It's one of the most important things you can ever do.

Discover the Illusion.

Facing the dragon may seem like a scary thing to do, but it becomes relatively easy once you discover that the dragon is just an illusion.

There is no such thing as worthy or worthless, good enough or not good enough. These are only judgments. They do not exist in the physical universe. They only exist in our mind.

You can search the whole world over for a "worthy" or a "good enough," but you will never find one. If you found one, what color would it be? How much would it weigh? How big would it be?

You can't answer these questions because worthy and good enough don't exist as things.

They only exist in our minds as thoughts, as points of view.

Notice that anything can be considered either a success or a failure depending on how you view it. Look at the chair you are sitting on. Is it good enough or not? One person would consider the chair good enough while another wouldn't.

To say that you are worthless is just a point of view. To say that you are worthy is another point of view. Neither are true. You are just you and nothing more.

The moment you decided you were worthless, or whatever your issue is, you created a mental concept or standard consisting of two opposite points of view, worthy and worthless.

You would then spend the rest of your life running from what you considered worthless, desperately trying to become what you considered worthy, all according to your point of view.

To say this another way, we spend our entire lives running from something that doesn't even exist.

Make peace with the illusion.

Although the characteristics that we run from are just an illusion, the hurt of feeling this way is very real. This hurt is also perceived as a major threat to our survival. "If I really am worthless, I might as well die."

We then go through life avoiding this hurt as though our life depends on it. We'll do almost anything to avoid facing this hurt.

It's the automatic, subconscious avoidance of this hurt that sabotages our lives. Every area of life that doesn't work can be traced to the avoidance of this hurt.

Fortunately, this is a hurt that can be healed. To heal this hurt you need to do the opposite of what gives it power.

Instead of fighting it, own and embrace it. Face the dragon and make peace with this aspect of you. As you do this, the hurt loses its power and disappears.

Face the dragon.

To face the dragon, put yourself in the hurt of feeling worthless or whatever your issue is. Then look over your life and see all the evidence to prove that you are this way.

It's not true that you are this way, but on a subconscious, emotional level, it is the absolute truth. It's this emotional truth that we need to face.

So put yourself in the hurt of your issue and see all the evidence to prove how worthless, not good enough, not worth loving or a failure that you really are. Every upset you have ever had will be more proof.

Allow yourself to feel this hurt. You really are this way. Let this in and feel the hurt willingly like a child. Then gently move to the place of "So what?"

While you are letting in the hurt of being this way, remember that you are also the opposite. You are also an incredibly wonderful, magnificent human being. Both are aspects of being human.

The more you let in the "fact" that you are worthless or whatever your issue is, the more impossible it is to fight it. When you can't fight it, the hurt loses power and disappears.

Walk through the healing process.

Now it's time to heal your hurt. It's time to face the aspects of you that you have been avoiding and make peace with them.

To be most effective, get in touch with your hurt before you start the exercise. This is important because the healing needs to take place on an emotional level, not an intellectual level.

Now, recall the specific hurt that you are going to work with. Are you worthless, not good enough, a failure, or not worth loving?

Select the specific hurt. Then answer the following questions. Work with each question until you can say "yes" and mean it.

Take your time and allow yourself to experience the truth of each answer. While you are walking through the exercise, continue to let in the hurt of your core issue and look for evidence to prove that you really are this way.

- Notice the years and years of hurt associated with being this way. Isn't this a hurt that you would do almost anything to avoid feeling?

- Do you see the enormous amount of energy and effort that you have spent trying to avoid feeling this hurt?

- No matter what you have done to avoid it, doesn't this hurt keep showing up in your life, over and over again?

- Notice that the more you have avoided this hurt, the more it has been present in your life. Do you see that this is true?

- Would you like to heal this hurt?

- Are you willing to stop fighting it?

- Are you willing to feel all the hurt of being this way?

- Are you willing to feel this hurt, willingly like a child, and let it come and go?

- Can you see a lifetime of incidents where you have felt this hurt?

- Hasn't every incident been more proof that, down deep, you are this way?

- Can you look at your life and see a lifetime of evidence to prove that this is true about you? Let this in.

- Even if you hate that this is an aspect of you, isn't it still there?

- Do you see that by your resisting, you have only made your hurt stronger?

- Are you now willing to stop fighting this aspect of you and make peace with it?

- Do you now give this aspect full permission to be in your life?

- Are you willing to surrender to the truth of its existence?

- Do you now give this aspect full permission to be in your life forever and ever, to never go away?

- Are you willing to be this way, for ever and ever?

- Are you willing to be this way and have an incredibly wonderful, love-filled life?

- Do you see how much you have suffered trying to become the opposite, trying to become a certain way.

- Can you imagine the incredible freedom and relief you would have if you never had to be this way?

- Would you like to have this freedom?

- Are you willing to give up having to be a certain way? Are you willing to give it up forever, and just be you?

- Do you feel a difference inside? Do you experience more freedom and peace? Do you feel more able to be yourself?

Keep working with this until you get to a place where you experience a great freedom. "Oh, how wonderful. I'm worthless. What a relief. Now I don't have to prove I'm worthy any more. I can just be me."

So What?

So what if you are worthless or whatever your core issue is? What difference does it make? None. You are also the opposite. You are also an incredibly, wonderful human being.

What does worthless have to do with tomorrow? Nothing. Your dreams can still come true. You can still have love. You can still have a wonderful, exciting, adventurous life.

The characteristics you have been avoiding have never caused you any trouble. The trouble has been caused by all the things you have done to avoid facing this hurt. It's the fighting, resisting, hanging on, and withdrawing that have sabotaged your life.

Worthless has never caused you any trouble because worthless doesn't exist. It's just a thought. It's the fighting of this thought that creates the suffering.

As you accept the "fact" that you are this way and discover that being this way is truly, "So what?", you experience a wonderful peace. Your issue loses its power and you become free.

What a relief when you no longer have to be worthy, good enough, important, or whatever else you decided you had to be. Now you can just be you and being you is all you need to create a life of miracles.

To learn more about how to find and heal this hurt, get the *Mastery of Life Audio Course* and read the book, *Heal The Hurt That Sabotages Your Life.*

ACTION TO TAKE

- Find the aspects of you that you have been resisting. Then notice how much of your life has been spent trying to avoid them. Notice that by your resisting them, you have given them more power.

- Notice how much you have sabotaged your life trying to avoid this hurt. Now notice the freedom that you would have if these core issues lost their power. Notice how different your life would be.

- Worthy and worthless, success and failure, good enough and not good enough, are not things. They are just opinions, points of view. See if you can find one of these in the physical universe. Notice that you can't.

- These aspects only exist in our minds, but in our minds, they are very real. To heal them, we need to face them. Use this chapter to make peace with every aspect of you that you have been resisting.

CHAPTER 5

LET GO

At any moment, your life is exactly the way that it is. You are the way you are and the people in your life are exactly the way that they are. This is true whether you like it or not.

When you fight and resist the way your life is, you create a state of fear and upset that destroys your effectiveness and almost always makes your situation worse.

To handle a situation, you need action, not resisting.

If you could somehow let go of your resisting, you would restore both your peace of mind and your ability to see clearly. You could then take the action you need to effectively handle this area of your life.

You accomplish this through a process called "letting go." This inner technique removes the fear, upset, and tunnel vision that sabotages your life.

The moment you let go, everything seems to change. With the fear and upset gone, you become creative and able to discover solutions you could never see before.

To see how this process works, let's look at the nature of fear.

Fear is created by avoiding and resisting a future event. For example, let's say that you are married and that you are resisting the possibility of your spouse leaving. The more you resist this future event, the greater your fear.

As your fear increases, so does the chance of your fear coming true. You become threatened and hang on. This in turn pushes your spouse further and further away.

By avoiding and resisting this future event, you create a state of fear and upset that tends to bring you the very event that you are avoiding.

To have a fear lose its power, you need to do the opposite of what creates it. Instead of resisting the future event, be willing for the event to happen. You don't have to like it, just be willing.

Keep in mind that letting go is a just a state of mind. It is totally separate from your actions. Letting go is what removes the fear and upset so that you can see what action you need to take.

If you have a fear of losing your spouse, be willing for your spouse to leave. This doesn't mean that you will to happen, that you want to happen, or that you will stand by and let it happen.

Letting go is something you do in your heart. Be willing for your fear to come true, but in your actions, do everything you can to make sure it doesn't happen.

The moment you become willing for your fear to come true, the fear loses power. The tunnel vision disappears and you become able to interact in a way that creates love and greatly increases the chances of the person staying.

Here is another example. JoAnne was about to lose her job and was full of fear. When I told her to be willing to lose her job she became very upset. "What do you mean lose my job? I have four kids and no place to go." She was terrified at the thought.

The next day JoAnne came back and said she cried for hours and was now willing to lose her job. She didn't want to lose her job, but she was willing. She said, "Our family has been through tough times before and we survived them all. We'll survive this one too." Her face was noticeably relaxed. Her fear and panic were gone.

In her willingness to lose her job, she set herself free. She later reported that with the fear and upset gone, she was able to produce ten times as much with one tenth the effort. By being willing to lose her job, she was able to keep it.

To let go, give up your demands and expectations for how life should be. Be willing for life to be however it is and however it may become.

You do this by granting permission. "I am willing for my spouse to leave." "I give my spouse full permission to be exactly the way he or she is." "I am willing to lose my job."

Give up your rules for how life should be and make peace with the way your life is. Set yourself free inside. Then take whatever action you need to have your life be great.

To make the process of letting go a little easier, there are two things you can do. The first is trusting.

Trust that no matter what happens, you will be okay. Now this doesn't mean that life will turn out the way that you want it to. Life often doesn't. Trust is knowing that however life turns out, you will be okay.

When you know that you will be okay, letting go becomes relatively easy. As you let go, you restore your peace of mind, you take effective action, and life turns out great. This then reinforces trusting.

When you don't trust, life becomes threatening. You fight, resist, and hang on. You then make everything worse, which reinforces "don't trust."

Ultimately, trust is a choice. Trust is something you create. It's a declaration. "I will be okay no matter what happens, just because I say so."

Trust is also telling the truth. Look at your life. You have had tough times before and you have gotten through every one of them. If you are in a difficult situation now, this too will pass.

In terms of spirituality, trust that whatever happens is for your highest good. Here is a powerful prayer that you can use to help create trust.

"God, I give you my life, my heart, and my soul. I give you my relationships, my property, and my health. You can take them all forever. Whatever you have planned for me is fine. I trust you totally."

Life is only threatening when you are resisting something. So stop resisting and trust. Trust that no matter what happens, you will be okay.

The second and most important step in the process of letting go is to be willing to feel the hurt.

This is important because it's the automatic avoidance of this hurt that forces us to resist. The moment you become willing to feel your hurt, the need to resist disappears.

Whenever you are in a state of fear and upset, find the hurt that you are avoiding and dive into it. Feel it willingly like a child. Feel it because you want to.

To the extent that you are able to flow with life, you will be in harmony with the world around you and your life will be relatively effortless.

So, look over your life. Where can't you flow? What are you unwilling to have happen? What are you unwilling to lose? What are you avoiding or resisting?

Make a list of all your fears and all the areas of life where you can't flow. Then work with each item until you are willing for anything to happen.

Notice that your unwillingness won't keep a fear from happening. In fact, your unwillingness will dramatically increase the probability that it will happen.

Use the following steps to let go:

1. Find the specific circumstance that you are avoiding or resisting.

2. Find the hurt that you would have to feel if your fear came true. What would those circumstances say about you?

3. Dive into this hurt and feel it willingly like a child. Feel the hurt of the circumstances and the deeper hurt of feeling worthless or whatever your issue is.

4. Notice that you will be okay no matter what happens.

5. Be willing for your fear to come true. Actually grant willingness. "I am willing for you to leave." "I'm willing to lose my job."

6. Take whatever action you need to handle this area of your life.

Work with each item on your list until you are totally willing for each fear to come true. You don't have to like it or want it to happen, just be willing.

As you become willing for anything to happen, something very special happens. You become very thankful for the life that you have. You create the experience of love and life gives you its treasures.

By letting go, you create a life of miracles.

ACTION TO TAKE

- Make a list of all your fears. What are you unwilling to have happen? What are you unwilling to lose?

- After your list is complete, work with each fear until you are willing for the fear to come true. Remember that letting go is just a state of mind. It has nothing to do with your actions.

- If you have difficulty letting something go, find the hurt that you are avoiding. Then dive into that hurt and feel it willingly like a child.

- Trust that no matter what happens, you will be okay. When you trust, letting go becomes much easier. Trust, just because you say so.

- Go through your life being willing to experience whatever life has to offer. This will free you of the circumstances and allow you to gain strength and happiness from within.

CHAPTER 6

OPEN YOUR HEART

Love is the key to having a great life. When you feel loved, life is wonderful. You feel better about yourself and everything around you. You also feel better about the people who love you.

When we feel loved, we naturally return it. So does everyone else. Watch what happens when you compliment someone or say how much you appreciate someone. Notice how happy and empowered the person becomes. Watch as the person fills with love and gives it back to you.

If you want to have love in your life, the solution is simple. Open your heart and give love. As you give love, you receive love in return.

Unfortunately, expressing love is often a

very scary thing. We are afraid that if we open our hearts and express our love, we will get hurt.

Years ago we did a workshop for a group of nine-year-old girl scouts. As soon as we talked about expressing love to their friends, the girls became very uncomfortable. All of a sudden they wanted to stop the workshop and go out and play.

As we talked with the girls individually, each girl said that she loved her friends but was afraid to let them know. "If I let them know how much I love them, they'll laugh at me, make fun of me, and won't love me anymore."

By age nine the girls had already learned one of our culture's primary rules about love: If you don't want to get hurt, don't express your love.

We have all been hurt and it's no fun. To make sure we don't get hurt again, we make decisions about what we should do in the future. We make decisions like, "I'll never open my heart again." "I won't let anyone get too close." "I won't express how I feel."

These decisions become our walls of protection. They are designed to either push people away or hold ourselves back.

We think that these walls will protect us from the hurt, but they don't. In fact, they create more of the very hurt that we are attempting to avoid.

Notice how you feel when you are around someone with thick walls of protection. Notice how uncomfortable you feel. You don't feel loved and you certainly don't feel like opening your heart and expressing love.

People with thick walls radiate the darkness of non-acceptance. They destroy love, generate opposition, and get lots of negativity in return.

Your most powerful protection comes when you open your heart and express your love. Love melts opposition, creates harmony, and heals hurt.

Notice how you feel when you are around someone who is very open, with little or no walls of protection. Young children are like this. Notice how this type of person pulls love out of you. Notice how loved and empowered you feel.

As you open your heart and express your love, you change the world around you. You bring out the best in people and create a life full of love and joy.

Look in the face of someone with little or no walls of protection. What do you see? What are the words that you would use to describe this person? You would see love, joy, peace, happiness, aliveness, freedom, and spontaneity.

The words that you would use to describe this type of person are exactly the same words that you would use to describe the experience of love. The words are the same because love is what you are seeing.

Love is the essence of who you are. Love is your life force. When you allow love to come forth, you have life. When you cut it off, you have death.

Notice what you see when you look in the face of someone with thick walls of protection. This type of person is rigid and dead. There is a thick crust of hardness, anger and resentment. Beyond that, there is a tremendous amount of fear and suppressed hurt.

Walls of protection are designed to keep the hurt out, but notice what side of the wall is the hurt on. It's not on the outside. It's on the inside. Our walls of protection don't keep the hurt out, they keep the hurt in.

Walls of protection are like a prison that

keeps us away from the love and the happiness that we seek. The thicker our walls, the more we suffer.

So, what kind of life do you want? Compare the faces of people with thick walls and people with little or no walls. Which face would you rather have? Which life would you rather live?

If you look, there is no choice, not if you want to create a life of miracles.

To be free of your walls, to open your heart, and to be an expression of love, you need to be willing to feel your hurt. It's the avoidance of hurt that creates the walls.

How do you feel about letting go of your protection and allowing yourself to be vulnerable? Notice how threatening this is. Just the thought of being vulnerable is enough to reactivate old hurt.

This is the hurt that needs to be healed.

In our weekend workshop, *Return To The Heart*, we do an exercise that helps heal this hurt.

Participants put their arms in front of them and clasp their hands tightly together.

Then they imagine their arms as being their walls of protection.

When they are ready, they gently open their walls of protection and create for themselves the feeling of being totally vulnerable with no protection whatsoever.

As they open their walls and lose their protection, they allow themselves to feel all the feelings and emotion that get triggered. They feel their hurt, their terror, and they continue to slowly open the walls to their heart.

When their walls are totally open and their heart is totally exposed, they notice that who they are cannot be hurt. They may feel emotion, but they can't be hurt. Once they experience this profound truth, their walls of protection never again have the same power.

You can do this same exercise. The key is to actually create the experience of opening the walls to your heart, losing your protection and becoming totally vulnerable. Make this real for yourself and allow yourself to feel all the emotion that gets triggered. Try this exercise. It can be very powerful.

While you are doing the exercise, remember that to be vulnerable, you don't have to be a doormat or let the train run over you. You can still do whatever you need to do. You just need to be willing for anything to happen.

Trust that you will be okay, no matter what happens, and be willing to feel your hurt. Feel your hurt willingly like a child.

The hurt that you avoid is nothing more than suppressed feelings and emotion from your past. Every time you feel this hurt willingly like a child, a little more of your hurt disappears.

Be willing to be hurt again and again. The more you are willing to be hurt, the more you won't be. The more you are unwilling to be hurt, the more you will be.

Here are a number of questions you can use to open your heart. Work with each question until you can say "yes" and mean it. Dive into any fear and emotion that gets triggered and feel it willingly like a child.

Here are the questions:

• Are you willing to feel all your hurt?

• Are you willing to be hurt, again and again?

• Are you willing to let go of your walls of protection?

- Are you willing to be totally vulnerable, with no protection whatsoever?

- Are you willing to open your heart and express your love?

The more you open your heart and express your love, the more you make it safe for people around you to do the same.

The world doesn't need changing, the world needs loving. There are seven billion people on our planet and almost all of them are afraid to open their hearts.

We go through life with our walls up, waiting for other people to take the first step and express their love. Then, if we feel safe enough, we will open our hearts and express our love in return.

Unfortunately, almost everyone is waiting for someone else to take the first step, and few do. As a result, we live in a world where people go around protecting themselves instead of loving each other.

When your life is about opening your heart and taking the first step, you change the planet. You make it safe for others to open their hearts and do the same.

When enough people are willing to express their love, the rest of the world will follow. We will then have a planet that is loving and supportive.

The process begins with you.

ACTION TO TAKE

- Take a stand on opening your heart and expressing your love. This may take courage, but as do this, you literally change the planet. You make it safe for everyone around you to express their love as well.

- Allow yourself to be open with little or no walls of protection. Be like a young child and allow yourself to discover that the greatest protection comes from love, not walls.

- Be willing to be hurt again and again. Look for opportunities to heal more hurt. The more you are willing to be hurt, the less you need your walls of protection and the less you will be hurt.

- Do the exercise where you create the experience of being totally vulnerable with no protection whatsoever. This can be very useful in opening your heart.

CHAPTER 7

WATCH HOW YOU SPEAK

When you were born, you were a full expression of love, but you knew nothing about the physical universe. You then began the exciting adventure of discovering life.

As life unfolded, you made decisions about the way life is. You made decisions like, "I'm creative" and "I like myself." You also made decisions like "relationships don't work" and "life is hard."

You thought you were discovering the truth of life, but you weren't. You were deciding the truth for you.

These decisions, or points of view, then became like a computer program. They determine how you view life and how you interact with the world around you.

You automatically act consistent with the way you "know" life is. Life then responds accordingly and reinforces your truth about life.

If you "know" that relationships don't work, you will hold back and sabotage your relationships. Why bother to put out the effort when you know that relationships don't work anyway?

If you "know" that life is hard, you will expect effort and struggle. You won't have the ability or the desire to take the action you need to create a life that works. Instead, you create a life that's hard.

As life proves your points of view to be correct, you become more and more convinced that you know the truth about life. This keeps you from discovering that your life is your own creation.

You create your life through your points of view. Some points of view improve your life. Others do tremendous damage.

To have your life be as great as it can be, create a reality that supports you. Keep the points of view that make your life better and let go of the ones that don't.

What are the points of view that sabotage your life? What have you decided is the truth about relationships, about love, and about life? What is the truth about you? List every negative point of view you can find.

Here are some examples: "I can't handle money." "Relationships don't last." "I hate to exercise." "You can't trust a man, or a woman." "You have to fight to survive." "Life is hard."

Find your negative points of view. Then let them go. To release a point of view, all you have to do is say, "This is no longer true for me. I let go of this point of view." Say this and mean it.

If this is difficult, look for what you are avoiding. What would you have to confront or experience if you no longer had this point of view? What feelings and emotion would have to face?

We hang on to certain points of view like we hang on to people. We hang on to protect ourselves. We hang on so we don't have to face something inside ourselves.

So find what you are avoiding and face it. Face your fears and feel your hurt willingly like a child.

Continue to work with each of your negative points of view until you are free of every one of them. Then go through life searching for more.

Whenever you make a statement that says life is a particular way, remember that this is just your point of view. If the point of view forwards you, keep it. If it sabotages you, let it go.

Let go of all the negative points of view you can find and don't create new ones.

Be particularly careful when you are upset. Most negative points of view are created in moments of upset. When you are upset, you react very negatively to your situation. The points of view you adopt when you are upset will almost always sabotage you.

When you get upset, instead of making another negative decision, like "Robert is a jerk," say something like this, "Robert seems to be a jerk, but I'm upset and I don't know for sure."

Also, be very careful about how you speak. The more you speak negatively about something, the more that negative statement becomes the truth of your universe. Your actions then become consistent with that truth and life responds accordingly, reinforcing your point of view.

Look at the areas of your life that don't work and notice how negative your speaking is. Without knowing, you speak your problem areas into existence.

When you speak negatively about something, you lose your power. You convince yourself that you have nothing to do with the problem. You become a victim and you lose your ability to take action.

So don't speak negatively about anything. Don't speak negatively about yourself, about others or about your life, unless you want what you say to come true.

Every word you say is a prayer.

We go through life saying, "I don't have any, I don't have any." Then we stop and pray, asking, "Please, God, send me some." Then we go on saying, "I don't have any, I don't have any," and we wonder why our prayers don't get answered.

Well, our prayers do get answered. We're just careless about the way we pray.

If you want to be free of negativity and

have your life work, stop speaking negatively. If something negative slips out, say "cancel that."

Sometimes a situation can seem so bad that speaking positively about it seems like a lie, but it's not. There is beauty and opportunity in everything if you are willing to look for it.

Mary was a senior editor for a major newspaper until she lost the use of her hands due to an illness. For her, this was very threatening. She had to give up both her job and her career. She didn't know what to do and became very upset.

I then asked her to find the opportunity in her situation. At first this seemed absurd. There didn't seem to be any opportunity, but she kept looking, and finally she found it.

Mary had always wanted to be a guidance counselor, but she was so involved with her career, this was never a possibility. Now she could go back to school, get her counseling credentials, and do what she always wanted.

The moment Mary saw the opportunity in her situation, she became thrilled. Her circumstances remained the same, but her point of view changed and so did her life.

Every situation can be viewed as either a predicament or as an opportunity. Either one is just a point of view, but the one you choose will determine what happens in your life.

You create your life by the way you say your life is. So watch what you say. If you want a great life, don't speak negatively. Look for the beauty and opportunity in every situation.

ACTION TO TAKE

- Notice that your points of view are not the truth of the universe. They are just your truth.

- Notice that you always act consistent with your points of view and that life responds accordingly. Notice that you create your life by the way you say life is.

- Make a list of every negative point of view you can find. Then work to release each one. If you have resistance to releasing a particular point of view, find what you are avoiding and face it.

- Watch how you speak. Don't allow yourself to speak negatively about your life, another person, or yourself. If you say something negative, say "cancel that."

- Whenever you are in a difficult situation, look for the opportunity. It will always be there if you are willing to find it.

CHAPTER 8

LIVE AT CAUSE

At any moment, you are totally, one-hundred percent at the effect of the world around you. Whatever happens around you, you will react accordingly.

At the same time, the world around you is totally, one-hundred percent at the effect of you. Whatever you do, the world around you will react to you. This makes you the cause of what happens.

You are totally at the effect and you are totally the cause. You are both at the same time, but you only experience yourself as being one or the other.

How you experience yourself at any moment determines your ability to deal with life.

When you experience yourself as being at the effect, you have no power. You become a victim of your circumstances and get depressed. You lose your confidence, your energy, and your ability to take action. Life gets worse and you become even more at the effect.

When you are at the effect, all you can see are your circumstances. You don't notice that being at the effect is just a state of mind.

At any moment, you have the ability to shift from being at the effect to being at cause. You do this by generating a determination to handle your situation and by taking action. Notice that this is something that you have done before.

Find a time when you were at the effect of something and you decided that you had had enough. You reached your limit and decided to take action. You then grabbed your situation by the horns and started turning your problem around.

How did you feel the moment you became determined to handle your situation? You felt great. Instantly, you got your confidence and energy back. Fear and upset disappeared. You felt better about yourself and better about your life.

You also became very effective. Solutions appeared and the problem, which before was such a monster, was either resolved or at least, became very manageable.

The moment you decided to take charge of your situation you shifted from being at the effect of your circumstances to being at cause. You took charge of your life and your life started working.

Here are some examples to illustrate this concept:

Example 1

Jan had been unhappy in her marriage for several years. It seemed like she and her husband were always fighting. Then one morning she decided that she had suffered enough.

She decided that she would seek marriage counseling and if that didn't work, she would end the marriage. This was a simple plan, but it was one that worked.

The moment she became determined to handle her situation and committed herself to the plan, she shifted from being at the effect to being at cause. Jan felt empowered and was able to take action.

When her husband refused to participate in the counseling, She filed for divorce and got on with her life.

Example 2

Robert was a self-employed consultant. When he lost his primary client, he became depressed. Then one day he realized that no matter how he felt, his client was gone and now he had a choice. He could continue to be upset or he could start looking for new clients.

He let go of the past and decided to go full speed looking for new clients. He created a marketing plan and started taking action. The moment Robert committed to taking action, his depression disappeared and his confidence returned.

His marketing plan took a lot of work, but when it was completed, Robert's client base was larger than ever.

The key to living at cause is simple; don't stay at effect. As soon as you notice that you are at effect, stop. Stop being at the effect of your situation and handle it. Handle your situation as fast as you can.

Sometimes you need to generate a lot of energy to create the determination necessary to handle a situation. This is especially true when you are deep at effect, but this is what you need to do if you want your life to work.

Whenever you are at the effect of something, use these steps to return to cause:

1. Notice that you are at the effect of something.

2. Remember that you have the ability to shift from being at the effect to being at cause.

3. List the specific circumstances that you are at the effect of.

4. Generate a commitment and a determination to do whatever it takes to handle each item that you are at the effect of.

5. Take action. Do whatever you need to handle these areas of your life.

The more you shift from effect to cause, the more you develop your ability to make the shift. You soon discover that living at the effect is only a choice, a choice that produces needless suffering.

Practice making this shift as often as possible. Do this so you can master living at cause.

Most situations get resolved so quickly you wonder why you waited so long to handle them. Others take a little longer.

Some situations may take years to resolve, but the moment you commit yourself to a plan and you throw yourself into it, you shift from being at the effect to being at cause, and the suffering stops.

Most of the items that you are at the effect of are minor. Some are major, but all of them produce suffering. When your life is full of items that you are at the effect of, you suffer a lot.

What aspects of your life are you at the effect of? What aspects of your life don't work?

Notice how much you suffer by not handling these items. Notice how much these items drain you of your energy, your aliveness, and your peace of mind.

Each item in your life that you are at the effect of is an item that needs to be handled.

Imagine what your life would be like if you handled everything that you are now at the effect of. Take a moment and actually imagine this. Notice the incredible freedom and peace you would have.

ACTION TO TAKE

- Notice what life is like when you are at the effect. Notice how discouraged you become and how much you suffer. Notice how powerless you feel.

- Now recall a time when you shifted from being at the effect to being at cause. Notice how much better you felt after you made the shift. Notice what happened to the area of life that you were at the effect of.

- Are you willing to live your life at cause? Notice what a difference this would make in the quality of your life. Notice how much more effective you would be.

- Don't allow yourself to remain at the effect of anything. The moment you notice that you are at the effect of something, stop. Find what you are at the effect of and handle it. Live your life at cause.

- Practice making the shift from effect to cause. The more you make this shift, the more you master living at cause and the more you can determine how your life will be.

CHAPTER 9

CLEAN UP YOUR LIFE

The moment you are faced with an aspect of your life that doesn't work, you get upset and close down. You lose your aliveness, your peace of mind, and your effectiveness.

If you want your life to be as great as it can be, you need to handle the items in your life that don't work. In other words, you need to clean up your life.

The first step in cleaning up your life is to discover the specific items that need to be handled. What are the items in your life that sabotage your happiness? What aspects of your life do you get upset about?

Get a notebook and list every item in your life that you are at the effect of. List the big items and the small items.

List everything in your life that bothers you. Even if an item seems impossible to handle or it's something that you are not ready to deal with, write it down.

Use the following categories to make your list.

- Physical Environment

- Relationships

- Guilt and Wrongdoings

- Job and Career

- Finances

- Legal

- Health and Fitness

- Miscellaneous

Make sure every item of your life that doesn't work is listed somewhere. Be as specific as possible.

Physical Environment

Notice how you feel when you are in a car that is dirty and full of trash. Now notice how you feel when you are in a car that has just been washed and vacuumed. Notice how much better you feel.

When your physical environment is sloppy and cluttered, your state of mind will be clouded and scattered. A clean and orderly environment supports a clear state of mind.

Do everything you can to keep your physical environment clean and orderly. This includes your home, your car and your place of work.

What needs to be cleaned up in your environment? What aspects of your environment are you at the effect of? Do you have a closet that you hate to go into? Do you have a door that is always stuck? Is your car dented? Do you have a faucet that constantly drips?

List every item in your physical environment that needs to be cleaned or that bothers you.

As you clean up your physical environment, you will notice an immediate difference. You will feel more alive and have more energy. You will feel better about yourself and your life.

Relationships

Whenever you have a relationship that isn't working, there is a part of you that closes down inside. You become more defensive, your walls of protection get thicker, and you become less effective in your other relationships.

To create a life of love, get to the place where every one of your relationships is loving and supportive. To start, make a list of every person that you have negative feelings toward.

Who do you avoid or resent? Who can't you get along with? Who do you get upset about the moment you hear his or her name? List every relationship you have that doesn't work.

After you complete your list, start the process of healing each relationship. Read the next two chapters to learn how.

Guilt and Wrongdoings

Past misdeeds are like heavy weights that slow you down. They inhibit your aliveness, your self-respect, and your self-expression.

What have you done in the past that still weighs on you today? What do you feel guilty about? What are you hiding? What don't you want people to know about you?

List every bad thing you have ever done from the time you were born until now. Be careful not to lie to yourself. If you have a thought about something you have done, write it down.

After you complete your list, throw it away. By acknowledging what you have done and putting it on paper, you will heal much of your past.

Now make a new list of guilt and wrongdoings. This second list will be much shorter and will show you the items you need to work on.

Do whatever is necessary to free yourself from the past. If you have guilt for something, forgive yourself. If you have done something bad to someone, go back to the person and clean up what you have done. Offer to make amends and ask the person to forgive you.

If the person is impossible to find or is no longer alive, write the person an unaddressed letter or talk to the person in your imagination.

If there is something you have done that you don't want anyone to know about, tell someone. Tell several people. The weight of your past deeds doesn't come from what you did. The suffering comes from hiding, avoiding, and withholding what you did.

This doesn't mean call a press conference to expose your past, just be willing for everyone to know what happened. Keep in mind that everyone else has a similar list and theirs is probably much worse than yours.

Once you are willing for anyone to know anything about you, you will have nothing to hide and you will experience a profound freedom. Being free of your past will be an enormous relief.

Job and Career

We spend most of our lives in some kind of job. You may be busy earning a living or taking care of a family. Your job, whatever it is, has an enormous impact on the quality of your life.

Does your job nurture you and fill you with aliveness and energy, or is your job an emotional drain? Do you love your career or do you just endure it?

If you don't love what you do, you should consider doing something else. Life is too short to suffer. If you have the desire, you can find a job that empowers you

If your job or career doesn't support you, put this on your list of items that you are at the effect of. List anything about your job or career that bothers you.

Do you have projects that are past due? Is your paperwork a mess? Are there certain conversations you need to have but have been avoiding? List anything concerning your job or your career that you are at the effect of.

Finances

If you are frequently upset about your finances, you have a condition of suffering that needs to be handled.

Financial upsets seem to be due to a lack of income, but this is rarely the case. Most financial upsets are due to over-spending. When your expenses are more than your income, you can expect to be upset.

The key to prosperity is to spend less than you earn. If you are spending more than you earn, you may need to take some drastic action.

You may need to change your lifestyle and reduce your expenses. You may need to move or sell some property. You may need to find another source of income? What action do you need to take?

If you have past due obligations, contact the people you owe and give them a plan for how and when the debt will be paid. Making new financial arrangements can be a big relief. Make sure you keep any promises you make.

List everything you need to handle in the area of finance.

Legal

Do you have a divorce or a lawsuit that weighs you down? Do you need a will? Do you have any unpaid traffic violations? Does your driver's license have your correct address? Do you owe back taxes? Is your insurance in order? List everything of a legal nature that you need to handle.

Health and Fitness

What bothers you about your body or your health? Are you upset about your physical fitness or your appearance? Do you have physical ailments? Do you need a physical examination? Do your teeth need work? Do you need a new prescription for eye glasses? List everything about your body and your health that concerns you.

Miscellaneous

List anything else that bothers you but doesn't fit under another category.

After your list is complete, the next step is to handle each item. The process may take some time and some hard work, but the results will certainly be worth your effort.

Look at times in your past when you handled something that you were at the effect of. Didn't it feel great? Didn't your life become a more effortless and more enjoyable?

What would your life be like if you handled twenty percent of the items on your list? What if you handled fifty or eighty percent? What would your life be like if you handled every item on your list?

Each time you handle an item, you gain more freedom and more energy. You become more effective and life works a little better. Every step you take to clean up your life makes a difference in the quality of your life.

To be most effective, find a friend to work with. Make promises to each other about what you are going to handle and by when. A promise to a friend can give you the incentive to handle items you would otherwise put off. Group support is invaluable and can be a lot of fun.

You can create a life that is relatively effortless. You certainly have the ability. All you need is the commitment and determination to make it happen.

ACTION TO TAKE

- Get a notebook and make a list of every item in your life that you are at the effect of. List the big items, the small items, and even the items that seem impossible to handle.

- Handle the items on your list as fast as you can.

- Notice how you feel each time you handle something that has been bothering you. Notice how much energy and confidence you gain. Notice how free and alive you become.

- Find a friend to work with. Make promises to each other about what you are going to handle and by when. Support each other and have fun in the process.

- Make cleaning up your life one of your highest priorities. This is one of the keys to creating a life that works.

CHAPTER 10

BE FREE OF GUILT AND RESENTMENT

Guilt and resentment are states of mind that destroy love and sabotage your life. They seem to be caused by what happened, but they're not. They are caused by how you relate to what happened.

You create your own guilt and resentment. You can also release it.

Guilt

Guilt robs you of your aliveness, your confidence, and your self-respect. Guilt reinforces the feelings of being worthless and makes you feel undeserving. Notice the price you pay for your guilt.

We create guilt to punish ourselves. We think

that if we just punish ourselves enough, we will somehow make up for what we've done. We are our own judge and jury.

Maybe you have suffered enough. Ask yourself, are you willing to be forgiven? Are you willing to be free of your guilt? Have you been punished enough?

Select something you have done that you feel guilty about. Then use these questions to release your guilt:

- Did you do the thing for which you have guilt? Yes. Face what you did and let in the hurt.

- At the moment that you did whatever you did, didn't you have a very particular state of mind and didn't you see life in a very particular way?

- Didn't you act in a way that was totally consistent with the state of mind you had at the time?

- If you knew back then what you know today, wouldn't you have acted in a very different way?

- You didn't know then what you know today, did you?

If you were wiser and more aware you would have handled your situation very differently, but you weren't. You only knew what you knew.

Even if you thought you knew better, your degree of knowing wasn't sufficient to alter your actions. You certainly didn't know the consequences like you do now.

"But I should have known." Nonsense. How could you have possibly known more than you knew at the time? You had to make the mistake in order to learn the lesson.

This is the human condition. We have to learn our lessons the hard way. Notice how much wiser and more aware you are now. Notice that back then, you were doing the very best you could with the limited knowledge that you had at the time.

• Are you now willing to forgive yourself for not knowing, for not being wiser and more aware?

• Are you willing to forgive yourself for acting totally consistent with your limited knowledge?

• Didn't you do the best you could with the limited awareness that you had at the time?

- Are you now willing to forgive yourself for whatever damage you caused, as a result of your limited knowledge?

Five years from now you will be much wiser than you are today, but your future knowledge is useless to you today. Likewise, your present knowledge was useless to you back then. You only knew what you knew.

We go through life doing the best we can with very limited equipment. We think we know, but we don't. As a result we make mistakes. Sometimes we make big ones. That's how we learn.

- Do you now totally forgive yourself for not being wiser and more aware, and for doing whatever you did?

- Do you now let go of your guilt, just because you say so? You might as well.

Forgive yourself for everything you have done from the time you were born until now. Work with each item of guilt until there are no more.

Resentments

When you have a resentment, a major part

of you closes down. You become bitter and less able to express your love. Your walls of protection get stronger, your happiness gets reduced, and you sabotage your other relationships.

Ironically, when you resent someone, you are the only one who really suffers. The other person is out enjoying life, while you are stuck with your upset.

Notice the price you pay for keeping your resentment. Notice how much freedom, aliveness, and peace of mind that you have lost.

When you resent someone, you are saying, "I strongly dislike you." This destroys the experience of love.

The other person then gets upset and becomes resentful toward you. Then you resent the other person even more. Almost overnight, you create a cycle of conflict that produces tremendous suffering.

As long as you resent someone, a loving, supportive relationship with that person will be impossible.

We think that resentments are caused by the other person, but they're not. No one has the power to create a resentment in you. Only you can do that.

When you resent someone, you are forcefully blaming that person. You are saying that the other person is the cause and the fault. Not you. You are using your resentment to keep the focus on the other person.

We do this so that we don't have to look at ourselves. We don't want to see that down deep, we are the problem, that we are worthless, not worth loving, or whatever our core issue is.

It's not the truth that we are this way, it's just a hurt, but it is a hurt that is so painful, we will do anything to avoid feeling it. In an automatic, subconscious attempt to avoid this hurt, we blame and resent.

The moment you face this hurt and feel it willingly, like a child, the need for the resentment disappears and you become free.

So take a look, what is the hurt that you are avoiding? Put yourself in the hurt and find what those circumstances say about you. Are you worthless or not worth loving? Find what the hurt is and dive into it.

Feel this hurt willingly like a child. Feel it because you choose to. Then look at your life and see that this is indeed an aspect of you. Let it in.

By being willing to feel this hurt, you take the power out of your resentment.

The next step is to notice that the person you resent was doing the very best that he or she could with his or her extremely limited awareness.

If the person were wiser and more aware, the person would have been able to act in a very different way. But the person wasn't wiser, that person had a very limited ability. Notice how true this is.

Use the following questions to let go of your resentment. Work with one resentment at a time.

• Are you willing to be free of your resentment? Have you suffered enough?

• Are you willing to feel all the hurt associated with what happened? Are you willing to feel all the hurt of being worthless, not good enough, or whatever your issue is?

• Do you see that this is indeed an aspect of you? Let this in.

• Now take a good look at the person you resent. Doesn't this person have a very particular state of mind and way of seeing life?

- Doesn't this person act totally consistent with his or her very limited awareness?

- If the person you resent were wiser and more aware, wouldn't he or she have acted in a very different way?

- Do you see that this person isn't wiser and more aware? Do you see that this person has a very limited awareness?

- Are you willing to forgive the person for not knowing, for not being wiser and more aware?

- Isn't this person doing the very best he or she can with his or her limited awareness?

- Are you now willing to forgive this person for acting totally consistent with his or her limited ability?

- Are you willing to forgive the person for the damage that was caused as a result of this limited awareness?

- Do you now let go of all resentment for this person, just because you say so?

The moment you release your resentment,

you physically feel the return of your aliveness. You restore your peace of mind, your compassion, and your ability to love.

If you have trouble releasing a resentment, you are avoiding the hurt of being worthless, not worth loving, or whatever your core issue is. To release your resentment, let in this hurt. Keep working with this until all your resentment is gone.

If you still have trouble, forgive as a matter of choice. "I hereby release all resentment for the person. I forgive, just because I say so." You may need to do this over and over.

Work with this chapter, until you are totally free of all guilt and all resentment.

ACTION TO TAKE

- Make a list of everything you have ever done that you feel guilty about. Then use the questions in this chapter to be free of all your guilt.

- Notice that with each item of guilt, you were doing the very best you could with the limited awareness you had at the time.

- List the name of each person that you resent. Use this chapter to be free of all your resentment. Remember that you are doing this for you, not for the other person.

- Resentment is avoided hurt. When you are wiling to feel your hurt, the need for the resentment disappears. Find the hurt that is under each resentment and feel it willingly like a child.

- Notice that the person you resent has a very limited ability. Forgive the person for not being wiser and more aware, and for acting totally consistent with his or her limited ability.

- Work with this chapter until you are totally free of all guilt and resentment.

CHAPTER 11

HEAL YOUR RELATIONSHIPS

If you have any relationship that isn't working, there is an underlying condition of resisting or hanging on that destroys the love and creates your suffering. Here is how it works.

Love, by itself, is never enough to have a relationship work. The divorce courts are full of people who love each other. If you want a relationship to work, you need to make sure the other person feels loved, accepted, and appreciated.

This is true for any relationship. Whether you are husband and wife, brother and sister, or neighbors, the rules of relating are the same.

Every time you interact with another person, you either create love or you destroy love, and whatever you give, comes back.

You create love by giving acceptance and appreciation. When you give acceptance, the other person feels empowered and automatically becomes more accepting and appreciative toward you.

You destroy love by being non-accepting. When you are critical of someone, that person gets upset and automatically becomes critical toward you. Then you get upset and become more critical toward the other. Then the other person becomes more critical toward you.

Without knowing, you create a cycle of conflict that destroys love and creates suffering. If you have any relationship that isn't working, this cycle of conflict is present. If you want to heal your relationship, you need to end this cycle. Fortunately, all it takes is one person.

The cycle of conflict is like a tennis volley. Two people are needed to keep the cycle going. Only one person is needed to end it. When someone stops playing the game, the cycle is over. You stop playing the game the moment you let go of the resisting.

The process of healing a relationship is

relatively simple, but you need to take these steps:

1. Find and heal the hurt that fuels the resistance.

Ultimately, you resist because some hurt is being triggered. To find the hurt, identify the specific circumstances that you are resisting. What happened?

Then ask yourself the question, "What do those circumstances say about me?" Find the words of "not okay" that most accurately describe your hurt.

Then dive into the hurt of feeling this way. Feel the hurt of the circumstances and the deeper hurt of feeling worthless, not worth loving or whatever your issue is. Feel it willingly, like a child.

As you do this, the resistance loses power. You can then heal your relationship. This is the most important part of the healing process. Make sure you do it.

2. Give the person full permission to be the way he or she is.

Acceptance is nothing more than surrendering to the truth. That person is the way he or she is, whether you like it or not. Your feelings are totally irrelevant. Hating the way someone is doesn't change a thing.

When you are at peace with the way someone is, you can see what needs to be done.

3. Forgive the person.

Resentment is a subconscious tool that we use to avoid feeling our hurt. As long as you keep your resentment, you keep your hurt.

Whenever you resent someone, you are forcefully fueling the cycle of conflict. With every breath, you are saying, "I strongly dislike you." The other person then gets upset and gives it right back to you.

You suffer greatly when you resent. Make sure you release all your resentment. Use the preceding chapter to learn how.

4. Accept full 100% responsibility for the loss of love.

A cycle of conflict cannot exist with only one person. Two people are required. Once you see your role in the problem, you can turn your situation around.

Now this can be very threatening. We don't

want to see our role in the problem. If we are responsible, this would prove that we are worthless, not good enough, and so on.

In an automatic attempt to avoid this hurt, we blame and resent. Unfortunately, the moment we do this, we give the other person all our power.

To understand how this happens, let's look at the nature of responsibility. We have been taught that relationships are 50/50, but they're not. Relationships are 100/100.

Whatever the other person does, you will respond accordingly. If the person is loving and supportive, you will respond one way. If the person is critical or controlling, you will respond another way.

This makes the other person 100 percent responsible for the presence or absence of love.

At the same time, the other person is responding to you. Whatever you do, that person will respond accordingly. This makes you 100 percent responsible.

Both of you are 100 percent responsible for the presence or absence of love.

When you blame someone, you may be

telling the truth, but when you focus on the other person's responsibility, you can't see yours.

When you can't see your responsibility, there is nothing you can do about your situation. You make yourself a victim. You give the other person your power and you stay stuck.

Once you discover your role in the problem, you can do something about it. You can turn your situation around.

To get your power back, find your role in the problem. You do this by noticing the following:

• You did not make sure the other person felt loved, accepted, and appreciated.

• You were judgmental and critical toward the person, maybe even controlling.

• That person got hurt, put up his or her walls of protection and gave it right back to you.

• Your actions single-handedly created and fueled the cycle of conflict.

• Every negative thing that the other person

did to you was a direct result of the negative things you did to that person.

Once you discover your 100 percent responsibility for the loss of love in your relationship, you can no longer blame the other person and the healing process takes a major step forward.

5. Let the person go.

When you hang on to someone, you create an environment where the person feels controlled and suffocated. You force the person to fight for breathing room. You push the person away.

So, for the sake of your relationship and your sanity, if you have been hanging on to someone, let the person go. You don't have to like it or want it to happen. Just be willing.

To be willing, find the hurt that would get triggered if the person left. What would those circumstances say about you? For most people, this is the hurt of feeling worthless and not worth loving. Feel this hurt and own this part of you.

When you are genuinely willing to lose someone, you dramatically increase the chances of the person staying.

6. See that you are just like the other person.

Any characteristic that you can't stand in another person is an aspect of you that you can't stand in yourself.

Would it be painful if you were just like this person? If this is an uncomfortable thought, this is an aspect of you that you are not at peace with.

You may not have done the same things that this person has done, but the characteristic is still in you. It's in all of us. It's part of being human.

Notice that this characteristic is indeed an aspect of you. You don't have to like it, just own it.

Once you own this characteristic, your resistance towards the other person gets replaced with compassion. You also become more at peace with yourself.

7. See that under all the upset and hurt, you still love the person

Love never goes away. It just gets buried by all the hurt. Notice that under all your hurt, you still love the person. You may not want to spend time with the person, but notice that the love is still there.

When you act out of the love, you create more love. When you act out of the fear and upset, you create more fear and upset.

8. Get with the person and clean up your relationship.

The next step is to get with the person. Tell the person that you've had some major self-discoveries and that you want to clean up your relationship.

Take full responsibility for what happened and ask the person to please forgive you. If you have been hanging on, give the person freedom to leave.

Say whatever you need to say to clean up your relationship. Then follow your statement up with action. Make sure the other person always feels loved, accepted, and appreciated.

If you want to learn more about relationships, get the *Mastery of Life Audio Course* and read the book, *How To Heal A Painful Relationship*.

ACTION TO TAKE

- Make a list of every relationship you have that doesn't work. Who don't you get along with? Who do you avoid or resent? List the name of every person with whom you are upset.

- Notice how much you suffer when your relationships don't work. Notice what happens to your aliveness and your peace of mind.

- Are you willing to heal all your relationships and restore the love in each one? If not, what are you avoiding? Is your avoidance worth the price you pay?

- Use the steps in this chapter to heal all your relationships. Work with this until you feel love for everyone.

- Make sure all the people in your life feel loved, accepted, and appreciated. Give up your rules for how people should be and see the love and beauty in everyone, just the way they are.

CHAPTER 12

BE PROSPEROUS

Most of us sabotage our own prosperity. We limit our financial growth and we set up ourselves for frequent upset.

We think that the problem is the lack of income, but this is seldom the case. Most of the people in this world would love to have your level of income. The problem is how we handle the income that we have.

We overspend. We use every resource available to raise our standard of living, and when credit is available, we use that too. The result is a lifestyle where expenses equal or exceed our income.

When this happens, you can expect to be upset. No matter what your income is, you will never have enough. You will constantly experience fear and insufficiency. This experience of lack then creates more lack.

True prosperity is created by two things:

• Being free of the fear and upset that comes from overspending.

• Appreciating what you have.

Imagine what your finances would be like if your expenses where always 10 percent less than your income. What would your life be like if you took 10 percent of everything you earned from the time you were 18 and invested it wisely?

You would be very wealthy and your prosperity consciousness would be one of abundance instead of lack.

If you could somehow set up your affairs so that your expenses were ten per cent less than your income, you would have a very different life.

But this isn't the way we handle our financial affairs. Instead of spending less than we earn and investing the rest, we overspend.

We overspend so we can get more of what we want. We are driven by our wants. No matter what we have, we still want more. Our wants are insatiable.

If you made a list of everything you wanted and received everything on your list, before long, you would have a new list of wants.

You can never get enough of what you want because the void you are trying to fill isn't outside of yourself. It's inside. We are trying force life to be a certain way so that we don't have to feel a very specific hurt.

Until you heal this hurt, you will continue to overspend. You will sacrifice both your happiness and your prosperity in a useless attempt to get what you want.

Instead of building an estate and creating a life of abundance, you will overspend and create a life of fear, upset, and lack.

To heal this inner void, you need to find and heal the hurt that drives your insatiable wants. This is the first step in creating prosperity consciousness.

Find the hurt that fuels your overspending.

The hurt that drives your overspending will always be some form of feeling not okay. For example, to avoid the hurt of failure, one person would overspend to feel like a success. Another person would overspend to avoid the hurt of feeling worthless.

Unfortunately, the feeling of success or worthy is only temporary. When you have trouble paying the bills, the hurt that you have been avoiding comes back even stronger than before.

To find your hurt, notice the feelings and emotion that would be triggered if you had to substantially reduce your standard of living. What would you have to feel if you lost everything?

What would it say about you if you lost your job, your home, and all your possessions? Would you have to face being a failure, worthless, or not good enough? Find the word or words that hurt the most.

Then allow yourself to feel the hurt of being this way. Feel it willingly like a child. Then look in your life and see all the evidence to prove that this is indeed an aspect of you. Let it in.

While you are facing this hurt, remember that this is only one side of the coin. You are also the opposite. You are also very worthy, more than good enough, and a great success.

As you let in the hurt that you have been avoiding, it loses power.

Keep working with this until you can honestly say, "Yes, this is an aspect of me. So what?" Then be willing to lose everything.

Be willing to lose everything.

If you can have nothing and still be happy, you will have control over both your wants and your spending. You will be more creative, more effective, and more able to have your financial dreams come true.

Are you willing to have nothing? Are you willing to be homeless? What would you have to experience if you lost everything? What would this say about you?

Find the hurt that you are avoiding and be willing to feel it. Continue to work with this, until you can have nothing and still be happy.

Once you are truly willing to lose everything, something very special happens. You become very thankful for everything you have. You then experience true prosperity.

This experience of abundance then creates more abundance.

Create a plan to reduce your expenses.

Once you are willing to lose everything, the next step is to create a plan for how you will lower your expenses.

What do you need to do to make sure your expenses are at least 10 per cent less than your income? Do you need to move your residence or sell some property? Do you need to restructure your debt? What steps do you need to take?

The moment you create a plan and commit to it, you get power over your situation. You still may have lots of work to do, but committing to a plan gives you the sense that this area of your life is now handled.

ACTION TO TAKE

- Notice the damage overspending has caused in your life. Notice the fear, the upset, and the feelings of lack that come from overspending.

- Find the core issue that fuels your insatiable wants and causes your overspending. Find what you would have to experience about yourself if you lost everything. Then make peace with that aspect of you.

- Be willing to have nothing and appreciate everything that you have. Work with this until you can live in poverty and still be happy. Then notice the abundance that you already have in your life. Be very thankful for everything you have.

- Set up your financial affairs so that you spend at least ten per cent less than you earn. Take the remaining ten per cent and invest it wisely. Create a plan for how you will accomplish this.

- Lead a simple life that works. Don't overspend.

CHAPTER 13

GO FOR YOUR DREAMS

When you have something to go for, life becomes an exciting adventure. You have direction and purpose, a reason to wake up in the morning.

When you have nothing to go for, life feels empty, meaningless and not much fun. So, if you don't have something to go for, find something. Find it as fast as you can.

What are your dreams? What do you want in life? What possibility can you get excited about?

To start the process of discovering what you want, take a few minutes and imagine your ideal life. How do you want your life to be? What do you want to accomplish? What do you want to have?

Do some daydreaming and write down what you see. Describe your ideal life in detail. Be as specific as possible. The clearer you are on want you want, the easier it is to have your dreams come true.

While you are writing, be sure and use the present tense. Say, "I am out of debt," rather than "I want to be out of debt." Keep writing until there is nothing more to add.

After you get clear on what you want, the next step is to have your dream come true. To do this, there are several steps to take:

1. Be willing for your dream to never come true.

2. Create the knowing that your dream is on the way.

3. Take action.

Be willing for your dream to never come true.

If you feel that you need something outside of yourself in order to be happy, you well feel threatened by anything that stands in your way. You will operate in a state of tunnel vision and you will push your dream away.

By being willing for your dream to never come true, you remove the fear, upset, and tunnel vision. You see life clearly. You become more creative, more resourceful, and far more able to have your dream come truc.

Create the knowing that your dream is on the way.

When you create the knowing that something is on its way, you change how you relate to that area of your life. You also change what happens in the world around you.

Opportunities and solutions show up. You gain a special confidence and you become empowered to take the action you need to have your dream come true.

Here is a simple exercise that can create this knowing:

Select the specific dream that you want to come true in your life. Do you want a new romantic relationship or a new job? Do you want to handle a certain area of your life?

After you select the dream that you want to come true, the next step is to create a burst of positive energy. Say, "Yes" with lots of joy, power, and excitement. This creates a level of energy where miracles can happen.

Then close your eyes and visualize the result you want to produce. Imagine that your dream has already come true. It's not something in the future. It's already here. Imagine your new life in lots of detail. Make this very real for yourself.

Now add a tremendous amount of joy to the visualization. It's the joy that removes your restrictions and limitations. So, create lots of it. Put a big grin on your face and create the feeling of being very thankful for your miracle.

Bask in the joy of your dream having come true. Then look at the circumstances surrounding your miracle. See if you can get some insight into how it came true. What were the steps that preceded it? Get all the information you can.

Continue this visualization exercise until you know that your dream is on its way. Then be still and notice what, if any, action you need to take for your dream to come true.

After you do the exercise, notice how differently you relate to this area of your life.

Take Action

You may not know all the steps that are

needed for your dream come true, but if you listen to your intuition, you will know the next step, and then the next one.

Each time you take a step, you become a little wiser and you get a little closer to the result you want to produce.

Sometimes you may stumble and fall. When this happens, pick yourself up and take the next step. If you keep taking the next step and never give up, your dream will eventually come true.

Go full speed to have your dreams come true, but don't get too serious. Treat life like a game and have fun. When you do this, life becomes an exciting adventure.

ACTION TO TAKE

- When you have something to go for, life becomes a lot more enjoyable. What can you go for in your life? What can you get excited about?

- If you don't have something to go for, find something. Get clear on what you want. What do you want to accomplish? What do you want to have? How do you want your life to be?

- Take a few minutes and describe your ideal life in lots of detail. Be specific. Do some daydreaming and write down everything that you see.

- Find what you want in life. Then do the visualization exercise. Imagine that your desires have already come true. Make this very real for yourself. Then add a tremendous amount of joy. Do this exercise until you know that your dream is on its way.

CHAPTER 14

FIND YOUR LIFE PURPOSE; SERVE

When your life is about serving, your needs will always be met. When your life is about obtaining your needs, your needs will always elude you.

Look at how you feel when someone is very giving toward you. Don't you feel like giving in return? Of course you do. Now look at how you feel when someone is always trying to get something from you. How do you feel about giving to that person? You don't want to.

The same thing happens in life. The more your life is about serving, the more life takes care of you. When your life is about getting, life takes away from you.

So have your life be about serving. When your life is about serving, your ego loses power and you become an expression of love. You feel empowered. You feel fulfilled and great things happen around you.

Ultimately, serving is just a choice. You can have your life be about serving or you can have it be about getting.

Life is also a lot more fun when your focus is on serving. Albert Schweitzer once said, "Those among you who will be truly happy are those who have sought and have found how to serve." There is a profound truth to these words.

One of the joys of life is to find a way to serve that expresses the very essence of you. This is the essence of life purpose.

Everyone is created in a different way and each of us has our own gifts, talents and abilities. Life purpose is the full expression of these gifts.

When you are living your life purpose, you feel fulfilled. You love what you do and you know that you make a difference. Your life has meaning and direction.

Life purpose is also the natural expression of who you are. You are good at your purpose and you love what you do. It is the very essence of you.

There are two elements to life purpose:

• Life purpose is something that you are passionate about. It's something that you enjoy so much, that you would pay for the privilege of doing it.

• Life purpose is about serving. When you know that your work makes a difference, you have the power to move mountains. Serving is what gives power to your passion.

Until you find your life purpose, there will always seem to be something missing.

Unfortunately, finding your life purpose is much easier said than done. You can't go to the library and look it up. You won't find it in the want ads.

Life purpose is something you create. It's something you bring forth out of your commitment and determination.

Although you can't look up purpose, there is a path where life purpose can be discovered.

The first step on this path is to find your passion. What do you love to do? What are you naturally good at? What turns you on? What could you throw your heart and soul into?

The process of discovering your passion can take months of active looking, so be patient and keep looking. You can use the questions at the end of this chapter to start you on the path.

After you find your passion, the next step is to find a way to live your passion full time and still pay the bills. This may seem impossible but it's not. There is a way to do what you love. Your job is to discover how.

Constantly ask yourself the question, "How can I earn a living doing what I love?" Explore every possibility and turn over every stone. Keep searching for a way.

Pray for guidance and follow your intuition. Maybe you need to get a different job. Maybe you need to go back to school. Trust yourself. Keep searching and keep taking the next step.

The process may take years, but once you have the commitment to find and live your passion, you will eventually find a way.

Once you find a way to earn a living doing what you love, your life will never be the same. You will spend the rest of your life having fun instead of working.

You also become very effective at what you do, and eventually, if you want, you can provide a good income for yourself.

Use the following questions to gain insight into your life purpose. Write down every thought you have in response to the questions. Let the words flow. Keep writing until there is no more response.

• What are you good at? What are your gifts, your talents and your abilities?

• What do you love to do? What makes you come alive?

• What were you doing when you were the happiest?

• What have you done that you are proud of?

• What aspects or characteristics of you are you proud of?

• When you were young, what did you want to be when you grew up?

- When you are on your deathbed, what would you regret not having done?

- If you could make any contribution to the world, what would it be?

- What is your passion?

- What is your contribution?

- What is your life purpose?

Keep looking for your passion and the contribution you want to make to the world. By doing what you love and finding how to serve, you add a very special joy to life.

ACTION TO TAKE

- Start the process of finding and living your life purpose. The process begins the moment you start looking. Your commitment and determination will show you the way.

- Use the questions in this chapter to gain more insight into your life purpose. Write down every thought you have in response to the questions. Keep writing until there is no more response. Use the questions to bring forth desires and insights that are deep inside.

- The process of finding and living your life purpose can take years. Be patient and at the same time, don't ever stop. Follow your intuition and keep taking the next step.

- Have your life be about serving instead of getting.

CHAPTER 15

EXPERIENCE YOUR SPIRITUALITY

In one of our workshops, we do an acknowledgement exercise where participants create a cycle of loving, supporting, and empowering each other. Then they walk though a process where they actually experience seeing God in each other.

The result is a very profound state of oneness. People experience a connection with each other and with life that is beyond words. Upsets and problems disappear. All that exists is a deep state of love, freedom, and peace.

Then we look at the nature of this state. People discover that, in this state, the circumstances of life have no power. Fear and upset cannot exist. Judgment disappears and the past has no relevance. Even the ego and the concept "me" disappear. All that exists is love.

When you live in this state of love, you are happy, alive, and free. You can flow with whatever happens. You are confident, creative, and very effective. Great things happen.

As you experience this state, you connect with a power much greater than you. You feel guided and taken care of.

The Bible refers to this state as "of the spirit." When you are in this state of oneness, you are living in the light and life works effortlessly. This is the domain of love, joy, peace, and miracles.

Living in this state is the essence and purpose of spirituality.

The opposite state is one of separateness. When we are in this state, all the focus is on the circumstances of life. We are convinced that happiness comes from outside of ourselves.

We then go through life trying to force life to be a certain way. We fight, resist, hang on, and withdraw. Instead of creating the happiness that we seek, we destroy love and create a life of fear, upset, and suffering.

The Bible refers to this state as "of the world." When you are in this state, you are living in the darkness.

Although both states are always present, you have a choice as to which one you live in. You can either live in the light or you can live in the darkness. Obviously, the opportunity of life is to learn to live in the light.

There are two states, but more accurately, there are two different directions. One is toward God and the light. The other is toward the circumstances.

One way to think of God is to imagine a white light that radiates outward. As this white light gets refracted, it splits into all the colors of the rainbow.

In the same way, God radiates outward and is expressed in all the different circumstances and variations of our lives. This white light, or God, is the source of everything.

The closer you are to this light, the more your life works and the more your life becomes full of love and miracles. The further you get from this light, the more you enter the darkness and the more you suffer.

The opportunity of life is to go towards the light and to connect with your life force. To do this, there are several important steps:

1. *Let go of the circumstances.*

When you hang on to the circumstances, you create a state of fear, upset, and tunnel vision that keeps you in the darkness and creates more suffering.

As you give up your demands and expectations for how life should be and flow with the way life is, you gain peace of mind. In this peace, solutions appear and problem areas clear up.

To make letting go easier, trust. Trust that you will be okay no matter what happens. Then give your life to God.

I have a prayer, "God, I give you my life, my heart and my soul. I give you my relationships, my prosperity, my possessions, and my health. I give you everything. Whatever you have in store for me is fine. I trust you totally. What do you want me to do?"

This is perfect peace. As you give your life to God and become willing for anything to happen, you can't help but live in the experience of love. You will then be guided to a life that will exceed your dreams.

2. If you don't have a relationship with God, make sure you get one.

For years, I had a prayer. "Take me, God, I'm yours. Take me, God, I'm yours." I would say this over and over, always adding at the end, "If you are there."

I didn't know if there was a God, but if there was, I wanted God to take me. Eventually, my prayers were answered.

So, give your life to God and ask for a relationship.

The process of creating this relationship starts with the desire and a little action. Imagine yourself in a room with a bunch of people. Then you notice someone on the other side of the room that you would like to meet.

Now you have a choice. You can either wait for that person to come to you or you can take the initiative and introduce yourself.

The same thing is true if you want a relationship with God. You are going to have to take the initiative. If you wait for God to come to you, you can wait for very long time.

So, if you want a relationship with God,

ask for it. Keep asking and keep seeking. Eventually your prayers will be answered.

3. Find ways to get back in the light.

Find things you can do that will pull you out of the circumstances of life and put you back into the light.

This is important because as long as you live in a world of circumstances, you are going to get caught up in the world around you. The moment this happens, you lose sight of who you are and you enter the world of fear, upset, and suffering.

When you have ways to get back into the light, you will be able to maintain the connection with God and your life will continue to work.

Some people stay connected by praying, meditating or attending religious services. Others get restored by listening to music, reading, being in nature, or doing yoga.

I make the connection by attending a small Catholic mass. During the mass, I go into a meditative state and experience the presence of God. I also listen to Gregorian chants and other types of music.

What are the activities that put you back in the light? Find what they are and do them as often as possible. Making this connection is like recharging the batteries to your soul. It's one of the keys to having life work.

4. Pray.

Prayer is very important because it does two things. It keeps your relationship with God alive and it produces miracles in your life. There are all sorts of studies proving the power of prayer. Prayer works.

Basically, prayer is having a conversation with God. Share your fears and concerns. Give your life to God. Ask for what you need and thank him for the gifts that you receive.

In addition to talking with God, it's important to listen. One of the best ways to hear the voice of God is to listen to your intuition.

When you listen to your intuition, you are receiving guidance from a power much wiser than you. This power has your best interest in mind and it will always lead you in the direction that you need to go.

Your intuition shows up as an inner knowing. It's often referred to as a "gut feeling."

It is very different from the voice from your head. The voice from your head comes from your past. When you listen to this voice, you are guaranteed to carry the past into your future.

Intuition comes more from your heart and it always guides you in the direction of love. So listen to your heart and do what it says. The more you listen to your intuition and do what it says, the louder it speaks.

Another great way to listen to God is to meditate. You hear God most clearly when you are still and have peace of mind.

When your mind is racing, you can't hear that voice from within. So learn to still your mind. You can do this through meditation.

There are many ways to meditate. One way is to get in a comfortable position, close your eyes, and create the feeling of joy. Then bask in the love and the presence of God. Allow your thoughts to have their say, and then be still. Move toward the silence.

In the silence you can communicate. Speak to God and listen for the response. Listen for your guidance.

Here are some very special messages that

were received in meditation:

The first message is from my brother. One day, while he was praying, he felt something take his hand and lead him to his desk. He then wrote a letter, but he wasn't the author.

Here is the letter:

"Trust me. I will guide you. You don't know and I do. I love you more than you know. I am the source of all you desire. You can only succeed by surrendering to my will. You think you know the way, but you don't. Learn to listen to me. Only I am the source of joy and fulfillment. You will never truly get what you want on your own. I am what your heart yearns for. Serve me."

This letter speaks a very profound truth. We think we know the way, but we don't. By giving your life to God and listening to God's guidance, you can be led to a life of joy and fulfillment.

Here is another message that was received in a meditation:

"I wait upon you. For I know within your heart is the desire to know me and I am always here. When the desire to know me becomes stronger than the desire to produce a better way from the self, then you will know me. But as long as you decide the better way, I will wait."

Ultimately, spirituality is just a choice, but is it is a choice that can change your life. If you are willing, you can be led to a life that will exceed your dreams.

You can have a life of love, happiness, and miracles. You can experience a confidence and a peace that you never dreamed possible. You can feel fulfilled and have a life of meaning and purpose.

All of this is possible when you put your focus on restoring love and connecting with your life force.

So let go and trust. Put your focus on seeking and creating a relationship with God. Learn to live in the experience of love. Follow your guidance and go for your dreams.

Everything is possible when you have God on your side.

ACTION TO TAKE

- Have your life be about moving toward the light and connecting with your life force.

- Let go of your demands and expectations for how life should be and flow with whatever happens.

- Trust that you will always be taken care of. Know that no matter what happens, it will be for your highest good.

- Make this your prayer, "God, I give you my life, my heart, and my soul. I give you my relationships, my property, and my health. What do you want me to do? How can I serve you?"

- Create a personal relationship with God so you can receive guidance and have your life be more fulfilling.

- Listen to your heart and follow your guidance. Pray.

- Find things you can do that get you back in the light. Do this as often as you can. This is like recharging the batteries to your soul.

CHAPTER 16

THE CHOICE IS YOURS

There are two different directions to go in life. You can either go for the circumstances, trying to force life to be a certain way, or you can go for love.

When your life is about the circumstances, you enter the world of fear, upset, and suffering. You destroy love and the happiness you seek will forever elude you.

When your life is about love, you create joy and peace. The world lights up around you and miracles become common.

We have been taught that happiness comes from outside of us. We then spend our lives trying to force our circumstances to be a particular way. We think that this will make us happy, but it never does.

True happiness can only come from within. You create happiness by letting go of your circumstances, appreciating what you have, bringing forth your love, going for your dreams, and connecting with your life force.

So now you get to make a choice. What is your life going to be about? Is your life going to be about forcing your circumstances to be a particular way or is your life going to be about creating the experience of love?

Regardless of what your life has been about in the past, what is your life going to be about now? Are you committed to the circumstances; or are you committed to a life of love, freedom, and inner peace? What is your choice?

As you choose love, you choose life. You also lead the way for those around you to make the same choice.

The process of restoring love begins with each one of us. Do what you can to heal your hurt and clean up your life. Be an expression of love and find your way to serve.

As you do this, miracles are guaranteed.

Thank you and I love you.

Bill Ferguson

This book is one that you will want to read over and over again. Work with the material and use the book as a reference. Every time you do, you will discover more about yourself and become more effective in your life.

If you want a telephone consulting session with Bill Ferguson or a member of his staff, call 713-520-5370.

If you want to learn more about love and how to create a life that works, attend our workshops, get the *Mastery of Life Course,* read our other books, and listen to our CDs.

If you are on the Internet, visit:
www.masteryoflife.com
www.divorceasfriends.com

MASTERY OF LIFE AUDIO COURSE

A step-by-step process for creating a life that works.

8 Audio CDs with Workbook

This course is about creating miracles. It's about learning, healing, taking action and developing the skills you need to have your dreams come true.

This course walks you through the process of healing your past, changing the way you relate to life, and creating a life that works for you instead of against you.

Topics include creating love, healing, restoring peace of mind, cleaning up your life, relationships, prosperity, life purpose, spirituality and much more.

This is a course that can literally change your life.

ISBN 1-878410-34-2   8 Audio CDs $95

HOW TO HEAL A PAINFUL RELATIONSHIP

And If Necessary, To Part As Friends

This book is also available on 2 Audio CDs

Paperback, 156 pages

In this unique book, Bill Ferguson shows, step-by-step, how to remove conflict and restore love in any relationship. You will learn what creates love and what destroys it. You will discover how to end the cycle of conflict, heal hurt, release resentment and restore your peace of mind. Bill's experience as a former divorce attorney provides rare insight into the nature of relationships. You will discover something about yourself and your relationships that will change your life forever.

ISBN 1-878410-25-3   Paperback..$15
ISBN 1-878410-31-8   Two CDs $22

HEAL THE HURT THAT SABOTAGES YOUR LIFE

Be Free Of The Inner Issues That Destroy Love And Create Suffering

This book is also available on 2 Audio CDs

Paperback, 144 pages

Ultimately, all of our suffering and all of our self-sabotaging behavior are the result of hidden inner issues from the past. These issues are created by the automatic avoidance of a very specific hurt. When this hurt gets triggered, it produces a state of fear and upset that destroys love and forces you to interact in a way that sabotages your life. Finding and healing this hurt is one of the most important things you can ever do. This book will show you how.

ISBN 1-878410-36-9   Paperback..$15
ISBN 1-878410-37-7   Two CDs $22

HOW TO DIVORCE AS FRIENDS

And Maybe Save Your Marriage

2 Audio CDs or 4 Audio Cassettes

This audio set walks you through the process of healing your relationship, one human being to another. You will learn how to end the cycle of conflict and restore love in even the most difficult relationship. You will learn how to resolve issues without arguing. You will learn how to heal hurt, release resentment and restore your peace of mind. You will learn how to communicate effectively and if necessary, part as friends.

Part 1 - End The Cycle Of Conflict. Learn how to end conflict, let go and restore your peace of mind.

Part 2 - Heal Your Hurt. Find and heal the inner issues that create your pain and sabotage your relationship.

Part 3 - Clean Up Your Relationship. Learn how to communicate and how to be free of guilt, anger, resentment and blaming.

Part 4 - Resolve Issues Peacefully. Learn how to resolve issues without conflict.

ISBN 1-878410-29-6   Two Audio CDs.....................................$25

ISBN 1-878410-24-5   Four Audio Cassettes $25

MIRACLES ARE GUARANTEED

A HANDBOOK FOR LIVING

A Step-By-Step Guide To Restoring Love, Being Free And Creating A Life That Works.

This book is also available on 2 Audio CDs

Paperback, 159 pages

This book shows, step-by-step, how to have love in every aspect of your life. You will learn how to heal your hurt and set yourself free inside. You will learn how to clean up your life and be free of upset and stress. You will discover how to take charge of your life, find your life purpose and experience your spirituality. This profound yet simple book covers all the steps to having life work.

ISBN 1-878410-38-25   Paperback...$15

ISBN 1-878410-39-3   Two CDs $22

TO ORDER BOOKS & CDs

ITEM		PRICE	QTY.	AMOUNT
Mastery of Life Audio Course 8 CDs and workbook		$95		
How To Heal A Painful Relationship	Paperback	$15		
	2 CDs	$22		
Heal The Hurt That Sabotages Your Life	Paperback	$15		
	2 CDs	$22		
Miracles Are Guaranteed	Paperback	$15		
	2 CDs	$22		
Divorce As Friends	4 Audio Cassettes	$25		
	2 CDs	$25		
	Subtotal			
	Texas residents add 8% sales tax			
	Shipping and Handling:			$6.00
	Plus 10% of Subtotal			
	Total			

Name (Please print): _____

Address: _____

City: _____ State: _____ Zip: _____

Telephone: Day: _____ Eve: _____

For Credit Card Orders:

Card No.: _____ Total $: _____

Exp. Date: _____ Signature: _____

To order by mail, send your check or money order to:
Return To The Heart, P.O. Box 541813, Houston, TX 77254

For telephone orders, call:
713-520-5370 or fax to 713-523-8412

To order online or to download any of our products, visit:
www.masteryoflife.com   or   www.divorceasfriends.com

Return To The Heart[SM]
A weekend workshop

This workshop is about opening your heart, healing and making a permanent change in the way you live your life. You will be more able to flow with life and more able to determine how your life will be.

You will learn how to find and heal the inner core issues that destroy love and keep your dreams from coming true. You will learn why your life is the way that it is, how to be free of the problem areas of your life, and how to have your life be great.

It is possible to have love in every relationship and in every aspect of life. We can show you how. Participants say that it is physically impossible live life the same way after you *Return To The Heart.*

Friday: 7-10:30 P.M.
Saturday: 10 A.M. to 10 P.M.
Location: Houston, TX
Cost: $325, $575 for couples

For dates and more information, visit:
www.masteryoflife.com
www.divorceasfriends.com
or call 713-520-5370

If you want to have a telephone consulting session with Bill Ferguson or a member of his staff, call us at (713) 520-5370.

You can find us on the internet at:
www.masteryoflife.com
www.divorceasfriends.com